CHRISTMAS SONGS
FOR CLASSICAL PLAYERS

ISBN 978-1-4950-9881-9

To access companion recorded piano accompaniments online, visit:
www.halleonard.com/mylibrary

Enter Code
2606-9394-4157-6936

7777 W. BLUEMOUND RD. P.O. BOX 13819 MILWAUKEE, WI 53213

Visit Hal Leonard Online at
www.halleonard.com

Pianists on the recordings: [1] Brendan Fox, [2] Richard Walters

The Christmas Song
(Chestnuts Roasting on an Open Fire)

Music and Lyric by Mel Tormé
and Robert Wells
Arranged by Richard Walters

Christmas Time Is Here

from A CHARLIE BROWN CHRISTMAS

Words by Lee Mendelson
Music by Vince Guaraldi
Arranged by Joshua Parman

The Christmas Waltz

Words by Sammy Cahn
Music by Jule Styne
Arranged by Hank Powell

Moderate Waltz

Jazz Waltz

Have Yourself a Merry Little Christmas

from MEET ME IN ST. LOUIS

Words and Music by Hugh Martin
and Ralph Blane
Arranged by Celeste Avery

I Wonder As I Wander
(Appalachian Carol)

By John Jacob Niles
Adapted and arranged by Celeste Avery

I'll Be Home for Christmas

Words and Music by Kim Gannon
and Walter Kent
Arranged by Brendan Fox

The Most Wonderful Time of the Year

Words and Music by Eddie Pola
and George Wyle
Arranged by Luke Duane

CHRISTMAS SONGS
FOR CLASSICAL PLAYERS

ISBN 978-1-4950-9881-9

To access companion recorded piano accompaniments online, visit:
www.halleonard.com/mylibrary

Enter Code
7778-3195-0006-2065

4

Clarinet in B♭

The Christmas Song
(Chestnuts Roasting on an Open Fire)

Music and Lyric by Mel Tormé
and Robert Wells
Arranged by Richard Walters

Rather slowly, steadily

Christmas Time Is Here
from *A CHARLIE BROWN CHRISTMAS*

Words by Lee Mendelson
Music by Vince Guaraldi
Arranged by Joshua Parman

Clarinet in B♭

The Christmas Waltz

Words by Sammy Cahn
Music by Jule Styne
Arranged by Hank Powell

Have Yourself a Merry Little Christmas

from MEET ME IN ST. LOUIS

Words and Music by Hugh Martin
and Ralph Blane
Arranged by Celeste Avery

I Wonder As I Wander
(Appalachian Carol)

By John Jacob Niles
Adapted and arranged by Celeste Avery

Clarinet in B♭

The Most Wonderful Time of the Year

Words and Music by Eddie Pola
and George Wyle
Arranged by Luke Duane

Clarinet in B♭

I'll Be Home for Christmas

Words and Music by Kim Gannon
and Walter Kent
Arranged by Brendan Fox

O Christmas Tree
(O Tannenbaum)

16th century Silesian folksong
Arranged by Richard Walters

Clarinet in B♭

Silver Bells
from the Paramount Picture THE LEMON DROP KID

Words and Music by Jay Livingston
and Ray Evans
Arranged by Luke Duane

Sleigh Ride

Music by Leroy Anderson
Arranged by Celeste Avery

Clarinet in B♭

Waltz of the Flowers
from *The Nutcracker*

Pyotr Il'yich Tchaikovsky
Arranged by Joshua Parman

Tempo di Valse

White Christmas
from the Motion Picture Irving Berlin's HOLIDAY INN

Words and Music by
Irving Berlin
Arranged by Richard Walters

O Christmas Tree
(O Tannenbaum)

16th century Silesian folksong
Arranged by Richard Walters

Clarinet in B♭

Piano

Silver Bells
from the Paramount Picture THE LEMON DROP KID

Words and Music by Jay Livingston
and Ray Evans
Arranged by Luke Duane

34

Waltz of the Flowers
from *The Nutcracker*

Pyotr Il'yich Tchaikovsky
Arranged by Joshua Parman

Sleigh Ride

Music by Leroy Anderson
Arranged by Celeste Avery

To Coda

White Christmas
from the Motion Picture Irving Berlin's HOLIDAY INN

Words and Music by
Irving Berlin
Arranged by Richard Walters